ALONG THE DARK SHORE

BOA Editions
New Poets of America Series

ALONG THE DARK SHORE

POEMS BY EDWARD BYRNE

FOREWORD BY JOHN ASHBERY

BOA EDITIONS • BROCKPORT, NEW YORK • 1977

Grateful acknowledgment is made to the following journals in which some of these poems or earlier versions of them first appeared: *Horizons, Junction, Pulp, Riverrun* and *Soft Stone*.

Typeset by Advertising and Marketing Graphics.
Binding by Gene Eckert, Inc.

ISBN 0-918526-09-4 Cloth
      0-918526-10-8

Publication of books and pamphlets by BOA Editions
is made possible with the assistance of:
The Literature Program of the New York State Council on the Arts;
The Literature Program of the National Endowment for the Arts.

First Edition: December, 1977

Second Printing, April, 1979

For Linda

CONTENTS

III
The Empty House

FOREWORD

The world of Edward Byrne's poems is our own world viewed through the wrong end of a telescope: curiously small and urgent. Tiny landscapes and interiors, almost inaudible sounds, minimal fluctuations of light and temperature form a backdrop against which the poet wanders, solitary among crowds. But the minuteness of scale is deceptive: "The crack in the teacup opens /·A lane to the land of the dead," in Auden's words. And in Byrne's poetry, not only to the land of the dead but to any state of momentous otherness. Particulars explode into universality as though through the action of a zoom lens. The atmosphere is as real and as fictive as the personage of the poet himself, suddenly emerging from the shadows with a brilliant image, and as quickly returning into the allegorical middle distance, strangely happy and at peace in this hushed, alien cityscape.

John Ashbery

BEFORE ENTERING
THE CITY

Harvest

Take this book

burn the pages
that do not have print

fill the spaces
between lines
with rich soil

on evenings of frost
huddle with it
beneath a blanket

nurse each word
in your seedbed

foster them
until mature

then harvest

and from between the petals
of each white rose
that sprouts

listen

for the sound
of steel on stone

Morning

It is morning

leaves are lifted by the wind

the road almost blue
between the red fields

far away
two headlights still flash
as if they have forgotten
something

My Voice

*If my voice dies on land
take it down to the sea
and leave it on the shore.*
— Rafael Alberti

My white voice
floats along the surface
billowing in the wind
like a loose blouse

the surf smoothes
the dark beach
with each stroke
of its green hand

the sky cloudless
painted sails burn on the horizon

ruins of sailors
illuminate the ocean floor

my voice speaks
less and less
as it begins to fill with water

disturbed by the tide
it rolls
back and forth
folding into itself
becoming smaller
shrinking until it disappears

leaving only
a white streak
as thin
as the wake
of a spoon

In a Room

In a room
heavy curtains are shut tight

people are sitting
in chairs that line the walls

there are no more seats
so I stand alone in the center of the room

the people are bored
and they begin to stare

I am embarrassed
my skin feels discomfort

I want to hide
but the room has no closets

at the far end
there is an empty coffin

I crawl in
and close the lid over my head

the people leave
dragging their chairs behind them

Waking

When I wake
you are asleep

your bare arms
tucked
beneath your head

a chill enters through the open window

I see the gray tree
where the moons nest

the walls of buildings
where the women wait

the sun still hidden
behind houses on the horizon

men rush by
carrying their clothes before them

the sleeves of their shiny jackets
old arms

waving

a tongue of green vine
slips through the split
in the window

there is a brown bird

the tender voice of the wind

a woman

brushing a broom
from side to side
against the sidewalk

tosses into the street
a trail of leaves
that edge the curb

like rust

a man passes

carrying over his shoulders
a saddle of black bones
woven together like water

crossing

under the crooked arm
of a streetlight

his shadow reaches out
to the woman

touching

shifting over her
like a stain

the sun rises

children run down the street
wearing bright bracelets

the automobiles shine
in the light

you awake and tell me
about a man
who can reflect the wind

who can tell you where it has been

who tells you
it arrives from another land

where he has been

where you will never travel

where there is a clear river
and a yellow steeple

and the bells
sound like stone keys
dropped into a glass jar

Explorers

Once again
    they cross the wooden sea
        the planks of their ships

knotted to each other
    like straw
        they sail in their own wake

each member of the crew
    mounts a mast
        to become that part of the totem

shaped into the animal
    he always wanted to be
        and above each vessel

lines of clouds stretch
    like serpents
        toward gray cliffs overhanging

a broken shore
    where the wastes of the sun
        lie scattered

The Desert

Everything is white

white eyes
white smiles
white faces

actors appear
from behind a curtain
of white sheets
wearing nothing

petals of stars
vanish
behind the white wall
of the sky

even the twisting weeds
levelled by the wind
seem to be composed
of sand

each day
the distance grows larger

the desert
extends
and begins to devour
the ocean

its thirst
enlarges
as it swallows
the salt of the sea

the sun draws nearer
encouraging the sand

bleaching all
with its heat

exposing
the dark comforts
of every oasis

Before Entering the City

i
Travelling the hours
before the blue dawn
I sleep
with both hands in my pockets

the passengers
are stiff laundry

hung from an old rope
swaying
in the cold

two soldiers debate
whether dogs or women
own souls

dogs lose out

ii
I awake
to see houses
jut through the snow

blisters on skin

white fields painted
across the fogged pane
have no dimension

once again
October has been buried
beneath an early winter

iii

The *Times* reports
of a farmer
in Kansas
who has been ploughing the snow

his neighbors
label him insane

yet they visit
each morning
to inspect the land

iv

I return to the window
and see the outline
of my own face

a bleached image

I decide
this is how I will appear
at my death

I am amused
as I watch others
peer
through their pale masks

into a thousand blind eyes

v

The daylight hours
shrivel inward

the peel
of a decaying fruit

yet the meat
becomes more tender

and the taste
sweetens

vi

The new coat
pulled around my ears
disguises the body
I have used for too long

the sleeves have been
sewn at the wrist

and the waist
tucked
inside my belt

a puffed bag
holding bones
and brittle muscles

vii

The train pauses
across the bridge
before entering the city

the sun is concealed
by clouds

slung across
the backs
of tall buildings

the sea has been filled
by feathered wings

IN THIS STATE

The Woman

For nine years
I had lived alone

sleeping
in a bed without blankets

each night
a visitor came
to sit by me

a small woman

fingering a rosary
and moving her lips
but saying nothing

each night
for nine years
she would wake me

I would ask her name

no response

I would shine
a lamp
in her face

but never recognize
the woman

one night
when I could not bear it
any longer

I moved
to one side of the mattress
to make room for her

she pulled from her purse
a pistol
placed it beside me
and left

I have never again seen that woman
I sleep without distraction

Another Day

I awake to the sound of a clock turning
like a key in a tumbler

I read the newspaper I have studied every morning
since her departure

through rain I follow a boy with a bad ankle
to the subway

and together we slouch against a wall
wet umbrellas left to dry

Mist

In the evening
mist swelled over the lake

lowering like a large body
that groans once

then twists its moist flesh
to the opposite side of the bed

November

Within a week
most of the boats
will be stocked
in dry dock

every item in their holds
removed

their portholes
covered by canvas

their hulls sanded smooth
and turned toward the sky

they will resemble
the freshly caught fish
the women carry home
to fry for their families

scraped clean
their insides emptied

Ocean Crossing

I approach the coast where the rivers are unraveled
curled inside my rubber craft   a fingerprint
drifting at dusk   crossing in an imprecise direction
hoping to discover a loose stitch in this seamless sea
a guest   wandering through an unfamiliar house
siezed with a sudden passion for cleptomania   wishing
that I could clean out the place   or at least
that I had a place to clean out   but there is only water
dragged over water   and the deception of the night
fitting its long body over the ocean   earth refilling
an empty pit

Returning

Dusk
    a starless sky
        the moon reflected
in the bones of a flower
    wisps of smoke
        rising
like gray hairs over wet snow
    branches bending
        over each other
men whispering
    hidden under heavy hoods
        I lean
into the wind
    and stumble toward the station

my long shadow
    a pencil
        across a leaf of paper
hunched under my backpack
    a hunter
        carrying a carcass
my shoulders aching
    beneath the weight
        my arms
stiff limbs
    of a frozen animal
        my black boots
spilling into the snow
    walking without a weapon
        the way barely visible
I hesitate

and wonder
     how it is
          that I am here
wandering through this whiteness
     that extends
          from one weathered building
to another
     I imagine
          how I must look
and smile
     at the sight of myself

a gray hand
     in a reservoir
          of milk

The Station

The station colorless
    the glass tracks
        shining
in the dim light
    there are no clocks
        the train is late
I have no idea how long the wait will be

a blind man
    cane tucked under his arm
        counts change
with his hands
    face and fingers

he stands by a window
    watching
        the empty air
I have left behind

In This State

In this state
governed by shoes

where the cornfields
are seeded with ash

and fear
salts the black snow

where all the billboards
have been covered by blankets

and even the debris
has been carted to a distant ocean

I have finally begun
to understand

that only those things we have forgotten
will survive

The Infant

Once a night
the dead man comes knocking
like a haggard dog
scratching the back-porch door

you know who it is
it is your husband

you know why he has come
he wants your child
his child

he wants
to take the infant with him

every night
for three months
you have refused
but he never stops

he wants to enter

he scratches
he barks
he howls at your window

you wish you were deaf
but you are not

so with nails and wood
you cover the cradle
and rock the coffin

Sestina

In the evening
I imagine men
moving down this street
toward the tall buildings
like mice
along a warehouse wall

but there is no warehouse wall
and though it is evening
there are no mice
no men
only buildings
lined along an empty street

so I imagine the street
to be a wall
on which the buildings
stand in the evening
like men
afraid of mice

and because the mice
have emptied the street
of men
and crawled inside the wall
until there is no evening
and there are only the buildings

I imagine the buildings
to be mice
moving through the evening
along the empty street
traps set behind each wall
catching only men

or I imagine the men
asleep in the buildings
and through each bedroom wall
the mice
gnaw holes to the street
and drain the evening

and the evening drowns the men
as it empties from the street into the buildings
and only mice remain along a warehouse wall

The Couple

She brought him a bed of stone
and he laughed

she poured him a bed of water
and he filled it with soil

she wove a bed of cloth
and he scissored it

she baked a bed of bread
and he ate it

she formed a bed of feathers
and satisfied he slept

she burned it

She

Sometimes she sits
in back of the house

pouring iced tea
from a yellow pitcher

staring at the space
where the trees once were

wishing
it was winter

The Old Man

The hands
of the old man
fall
from his arms

large-veined leaves
from yellow trees

his spine
as delicate
as a thread
of webbing

he moves forward
slow
unsure

in three hours
the war will be over

Your Father

People are pushed into doorways
by the wind

their forms
fingers
folding into a fist

                    *

darkness draws
like a slip
slid over a woman's head

we bolt the door
no one wants to enter

                    *

a man toddles past
wearing a gray topcoat
and no shoes

you say he's your father
but he's not

your father is lying
in a fighter
beneath the Coral Sea

your mother has shown you
the letter

                    *

you show me a family photo
in which you are sitting
at your father's feet

in the black and white memory
your father wears a gray topcoat

*

the man passes
without seeing us

we watch in stillness
two shoes in a showcase
waiting to be worn

Outside the Concert

i

Outside the concert
a man with scars across his wrists
is selling
the bottled blood of Christ

and we buy a pint

ii

Sipping from a flask
we place our canary
in a flute case
found in the attic

and bury it behind the music hall

THE EMPTY HOUSE

To Begin Again

The blue floor   a washstand
the window open   the sky
different
the river yellow   opposite
boys on paved handkerchiefs
strong dogs
quiet lines of sun
a donkey cart
traffic   horses   tourists
styles   expressions
workmen   a gadfly
hear the violins
two graceful women holding books
a gold clock
the blue day   august
late morning
I   silent   barefoot
faint ripples above the circle
in their bone gray windows   doorways
statues still rise
stone   river   muscular man
his short hand
on a woman's arm
her chin broken
I   face   tall
begin again
turning
yellowed covers

Waiting

I am
a stick of chalk
on a blackboard ledge

waiting

for a hand
or a filled glove
or a hook

The Empty House

Each evening you travel
to the empty house
of a friend

and mourn

offering your hands up
into the winter night
as if they were two lungs
that could not be revived

you stand
rocking in the cold

and not even your enemies
will admit they see you
as you feed your fingers
to the dark sky

you wear a white shirt
and a black overcoat

you eat the fruit
your wife had given you
to carry from home

and when it rains
you lie to yourself
about how the weather
could have been worse

the wind surrounds you
and burns the bare skin
of your face

and to remain warm
you remember
the women you have known

or imagine
the women you have never known

when the weather is good
you bring a book
and a loaf of bread

and you read between bites
because you read aloud

you have always read aloud

when you were a boy
you were told
that when you became a man
you would be mocked

because you moved your mouth
while you read

but now you are a man
and you are not mocked
you are ignored

and all night you stand

fingers folded
around the hard cover
of a bible

knuckles wrinkled

ten small faces
of aged men

and the bread you do not eat
you leave

a stone
on the lawn beneath the trees

to be finished
by blackbirds

and you can not sleep

because when you do
you dream

and you remember
figures

men with hands
shackled

a woman
screaming

bodies hung like wash

blind cattle
carrying bags of stone

soldiers
moving across a meadow
blotted by fog

collecting hands
in a basket

in the morning
your wife washes
the soiled cuffs of your trousers

and asks if this vigil
must continue

and your answer is that
among all
nothing else matters

and now you stand

a stone
on the lawn beneath the trees

among the blackbirds
that fill the branches
like dark socks

and mourn

and the empty house
is yours

and the wind surrounds you

and you stand pale and alone

in the past
you have always thought
that you wanted

to be alone

Birthday

Each day
we remove no clothes
from an empty closet

and wonder
if we are over-dressed

and we celebrate
as if it were a birthday

making wishes
and blowing out candles

and when no one is watching
relighting them

Along the Dark Shore

I walk
the dark shore
holding a dead crow
before me

it dangles
by a black thread
tied to its throat

this is how
I light my way

Edward Byrne was born in Brooklyn, New York, in 1951. A graduate of the M.F.A. Program in Creative Writing at Brooklyn College, his poems have appeared in various literary journals and have been anthologized in *The Return to Black and White* (Tidy Up Press, 1976) and *Intro 8: The Liar's Craft* (Doubleday/Anchor Press, 1977). He and his wife, Linda, presently live in Lake Ronkonkoma, New York.